THE WAR IN YOUR BACKYARD

Chicago, Illinois

Printed and bound in the United States by
Lake Book Manufacturing, Inc

10 09 08 07 06
10 9 8 7 6 5 4 3 2 1

**Library of Congress Cataloging-in-
Publication Data**
Spilsbury, Louise.
  The war in your backyard : life in an ecosystem /
Louise and Richard
Spilsbury.
     p. cm.
  Includes bibliographical references and index.
  ISBN 1-4109-1939-0 (library binding) -- ISBN 1-
4109-1970-6 (pbk.)
  1. Ecology--Juvenile literature. I. Spilsbury, Richard,
1963- II.
Title.
  QH541.14S6827 2005
  577.5'54--dc22
                                    2005009545

Acknowledgments
The author and publishers are grateful to the
following for permission to reproduce copyright
material: Alamy pp. 10–11 (Andrew Harrington), 28
(Andrew Harrington); Bruce Coleman Ltd. p. 13 (Jane
Burton); Buzz p. 12; Corbis pp. 4–5 (Clay Perry), 9
(Chris Hellier), 16–17 (FLPA/Tony Hamblin), 25, 29
(FLPA/Tony Hamblin); FLPA pp. 7 (Derek Middleton),
24–25 (Minden/Mitsuhiko Imamori), 26–27 (Brian
Turner); Getty Images pp. 8 (Taxi/David Maitland),
8–9 (National Geographic/Michael Nichols), 15
(Stone); Natural Visions pp. 22–23 (Francesco
Tomasinelli); NHPA pp. 18 (Stephen Dalton), 29
(Stephen Dalton); Oxford Scientific pp. 14–15 (Kathie
Atkinson),   28 (Kathie Atkinson); Photolibrary.com
pp. 11 (Dietmar Nill), 20–21 (Oxford Scientific/
S Kuribayashi); Photonica pp. 6–7 (David Cooper);
Rex p. 10 (Denis Cameron); U.S. Army pp. 19, 23.

Cover picture of an ant with a ladybird, reproduced
with permission of Corbis (Naturfoto Honal).

The publishers would like to thank Nancy Harris and
Harold Pratt for their assistance in the preparation of
this book.

Every effort has been made to contact copyright
holders of any material reproduced in this book.
Any omissions will be rectified in subsequent
printings if notice is given to the publishers.

The paper used to print this book comes from
sustainable resources.

Contents

Some words are printed in bold, **like this**. You can find out what they mean on page 30. You can also look in the box at the bottom of the page where they first appear.

The Life in your Backyard

There are many different kinds of animal in your backyard. Many animals crawl among the plants. Some animals live in water. Some animals dig down into the soil. Many of these animals are too small to see. Other animals only come out when it is dark.

These animals are all part of the backyard **ecosystem**. An ecosystem is made up of animals and plants and the place where they live.

Ecosystems

Backyards are one type of ecosystem. There are many different kinds of ecosystems in the world. Deserts, oceans, and forests are all ecosystems.

ecosystem   a place and the living things in it

◄ *It may not look like it, but a backyard is a busy world full of animals.*

A home in the backyard

Animals live in a backyard because it has everything they need. In a backyard, animals find food to eat and water to drink. They find a place to take shelter or to have young. All these things are **resources**. Animals need them to survive.

All the animals in an **ecosystem** need these resources. But the backyard may not have enough resources for all the animals. The animals have to **compete** for them. That is why you sometimes see birds fighting over the food in a bird feeder.

adaptation	body part or behavior that helps an animal survive
compete	fight with others for something
resources	water, food, and other things that animals need

Battle gear

Animals in a backyard ecosystem are like soldiers in a battle. They have to fight to survive. Every animal has **adaptations**. An adaptation is a special body part or a way of behaving. Adaptations help animals compete for resources and survive.

◄ A mantis has strong jaws to help it compete for food.

Backyard Battlefield

Different groups of ants **compete** for **resources** in the backyard **ecosystem**. Some types of ant will fight to the death over food or to protect their nests. Wars between two troops of ants are nasty. Battling ants grip each other tightly with their legs. They use their strong jaws to tear off parts of the enemy's body. Then, they spray poison into the wounds.

Ants work together to ▶ carry food home. Ants have a better chance of competing for resources if they work together. They could not compete as well if they worked alone.

The winning ants eat the bodies of the dead and wounded ants. They also take prisoners. They take young ants from the enemy's nest. They carry them back to their own nest. The young ants are then made to work in the new nests.

◀ A troop of ants has soldier ants and worker ants. Soldier ants have extra-strong jaws. They use their jaws as deadly weapons.

The Fight for Food

An owl has to **compete** for food. It hunts. The animals it hunts are called its **prey**. An owl's prey may include mice and young rabbits. Other animals hunt mice and rabbits in the backyard **ecosystem**. So, how does the owl compete for food?

This time the ▶ owl's prey is a mouse.

An owl has special **adaptations** to help it find food. An adaption is a body part that helps an animal survive. An owl has excellent hearing and can see in the dark. An owl can hunt at night. It sits and listens for prey. It hears a tiny noise. Then, its large eyes spot the animal that made the noise. The owl flies down feet first. Its hooked claws grip the body of its prey. The prey dies instantly.

Night-vision binoculars ▶ allow soldiers to watch things when it is too dark to see.

Owls don't ▶ need night-vision binoculars. They have large eyes to help them see.

11

prey   animal that gets caught and eaten by other animals

Diving gear

Great diving beetles are small, but they are as fierce as hungry sharks. Great diving beetles are **predators**. They hunt and eat other animals. They live at the edge of ponds and then go under water to hunt. Great diving beetles will hunt and eat almost any animal in a pond. Their **prey** includes insects, tadpoles, and fish that are bigger than they are!

The diving beetle is ▼ small, but it is a deadly predator.

Air bubble

Paddling fast

The great diving beetle has long, flat back legs. The beetle uses its legs to paddle. It can move quickly in the pond.

▼ *Scuba divers carry an air supply on their backs. Divers use it to breathe under water.*

Other predators hunt insects and tadpoles. So, how do great diving beetles **compete** for food? They have an unusual **adaptation** to help them. Before they dive, they trap a bubble of air beneath their wings. They use this to breathe. They can stay under water for a very long time. They paddle to the surface to get more air when their supply runs out.

13

predator   animal that catches and eats other animals

Centipedes crawl around ▼ at night looking for prey. Their jaws and claws are powerful weapons.

Tank tactics

A centipede is like a tiny tank. It has lots of legs that move up and down in waves. These legs grip the ground like tank tracks. The centipede can move backward and forward, just like a tank.

Tank warfare

A centipede is a **predator**. It uses the long feelers on its head to find **prey**. These feelers pick up the smell of insects, spiders, and caterpillars.

A centipede chases its prey over bumpy garden soil. A centipede's legs help it move quickly. A centipede's legs are an important **adaptation**. They help the centipede **compete** for food to survive. If a centipede loses a leg, it grows another one to replace it!

The centipede catches up with its prey and stings it with its front claws. This sting knocks out the prey. This keeps the prey still while the centipede's jaws get to work.

▼A tank's tracks grip the ground, just like a centipede's legs.

Eat or Be Eaten

Toads also have to **compete** for food. They hunt small animals such as flies and spiders. How do they compete for their **prey**?

The **adaptation** that helps toads compete is the color of their skin. These colors and patterns are the toad's **camouflage**. When a toad sits still on rocks, mud, or grass, it is nearly invisible.

Toads can sit still for hours at a time. They wait for a fly or spider to pass by. The prey does not know that the toad is there until it is too late!

Toads can also be eaten by other animals in their **ecosystem**. Hedgehogs and grass snakes hunt and eat toads. The toad's camouflage helps to hide it from **predators**.

Toad tricks

Toads have other ways of scaring off predators. They can puff themselves up, urinate, or ooze poison from behind their eyes!

▼ *Ambush! The toad flicks out its long, sticky tongue to catch a woodlouse.*

Stealth Fliers

Bats visit the backyard at night to catch moths and flies. So, how do bats **compete** for their **prey**?

Bats are sleek and dark. They are almost invisible as they swoop through the night air. Bats fly silently through the darkness. They make surprise attacks on their prey.

Bats can catch and eat ▼ up to 3,000 insects in one night!

echolocation   using sounds to find something

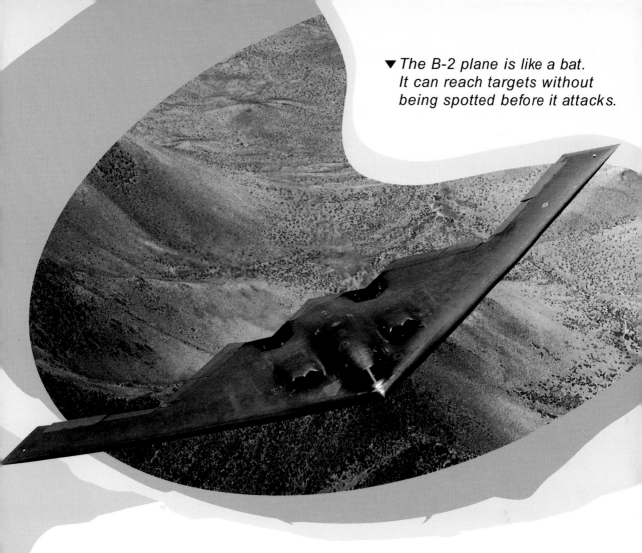

▼ The B-2 plane is like a bat. It can reach targets without being spotted before it attacks.

Bats can find prey in total darkness when other animals can't. Their secret weapon is called **echolocation**. Bats use echo sounds to find things in the dark. The bat makes high-pitched sounds. The sounds bounce off things near the bat. The bat's ears track the echoes. The bat can then figure out how far away things are.

19

There are lots of animals in a backyard **ecosystem** that would eat bats. A hawk could catch a bat and eat it. However, hawks only hunt by day. Hunting at night keeps bats safe.

Finding a Mate

Bats are almost invisible at night. But fireflies like to light up the night sky. Why do fireflies want to be seen?

Fireflies use lights to signal to other fireflies. Male fireflies flash light signals from the air to the females on the ground. The females then signal so that the males can find them. Then, the fireflies can **mate** and produce young.

The light signals are an important **adaptation**. An adaptation can help an animal produce young. Fireflies live for a short time. Males and females have to find each other quickly to mate. Otherwise, they would die without producing young.

Light-up time

Fireflies have a special liquid in their bodies. The liquid mixes with air when the firefly flies. This makes the firefly glow in the dark!

mate   when male and female animals come together to produce young

▼Being able to flash light signals is an adaptation. It helps the firefly to mate and produce young.

The Struggle For Space

You don't often see a robin looking this angry. The robin on the right is warning the other bird and trying to chase it away. The robin sings loudly. It ruffles its feathers and hops quickly toward the intruder. Sometimes a robin will even fight another bird.

The robin is guarding its **territory**. A territory is the part of the **ecosystem** that the robin claims for itself. This patch has the food, shelter, and water that the robin needs.

territory area that an animal guards from others

Robins eat berries and insects. In the winter, there are fewer berries and insects. It is important for a robin to keep its territory in winter. Robins with a territory have a better chance of getting enough food than robins without a territory. They guard the borders of their territory to keep enemies away!

◄ *Although robins usually look gentle, in a battle they will fight to survive!*

Parachute jumps

A mother spider lays hundreds of eggs at once. The baby spiders all hatch at the same time. This means there can be hundreds of baby spiders in one spot in a backyard. They would have to **compete** for the same **resources** if they all stayed in this spot.

The young spiders have a special **adaptation** to solve this problem. They use parachutes to get away from their family!

This group of baby ▲ *spiders is starting to float away in the wind.*

Traveling light

Baby spiders can float for many miles in strong winds.

▼ Baby spiders drift on the air, just like people using parachutes.

Each baby spider climbs up a plant to a high, sunny spot. The spider turns to face the wind. Then, it squirts several narrow threads of **silk** out of its body. The wind catches this parachute of threads. The spider is dragged along in the air.

25

Then, the wind slows down or stops. The young spider floats gently down to a new place. Mission accomplished!

silk   strong thread that spiders make in their bodies

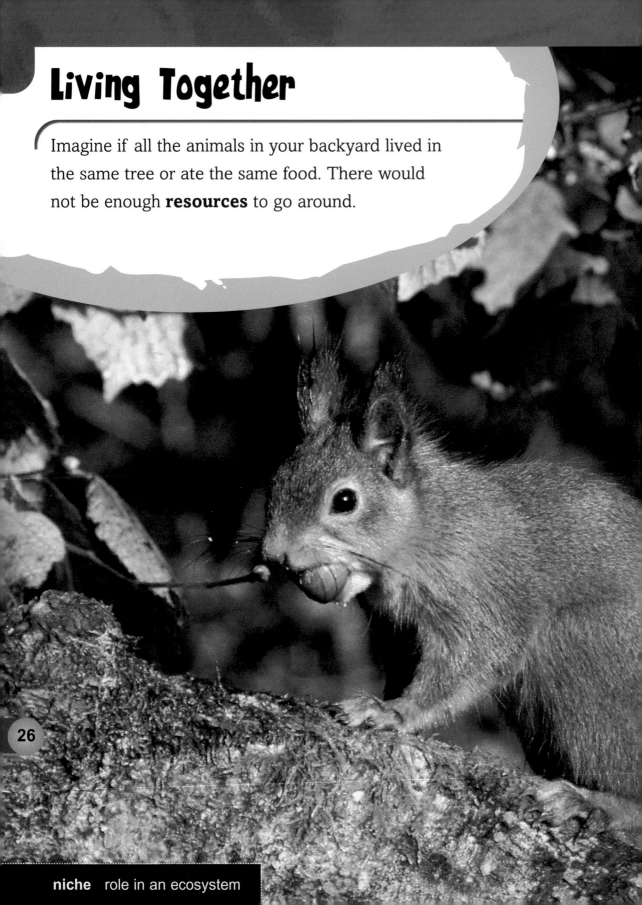

Living Together

Imagine if all the animals in your backyard lived in the same tree or ate the same food. There would not be enough **resources** to go around.

niche   role in an ecosystem

Different animals in an **ecosystem** live together because each animal has a different **niche**. An animal's niche can be the food it eats, the place it lives, or the time it hunts.

Animals with different niches don't **compete** for the same resources. Bats hunt in the air. Centipedes hunt on the ground. Diving beetles live by ponds. Ants live in the soil. Although owls and hawks both eat mice and rabbits, owls hunt by night and hawks hunt by day.

So, there's not always a war going on in your backyard!

◄ Squirrels eat nuts from trees. Squirrels may share the tree's resources with other animals. For example, woodpeckers eat insects from the bark.

Amazing Adaptations

Animals in a backyard **ecosystem** have different **adaptations** for survival. For example, centipedes have feelers that help them find **prey**. Baby spiders can float using threads of **silk**. These adaptations help animals **compete** with one another for **resources**.

◀Owls can hunt at night. They have excellent hearing and big eyes. They can spot prey before other night hunters do.

Diving beetles can▶ carry their own air supply. This helps them to hunt under water.

◀Toads use **camouflage** to sit and wait for prey. Camouflage also hides them from **predators**.

Bats can hunt insects in▼ total darkness. They don't have to compete with daytime insect hunters, such as birds. Bats also stay out of the way of daytime predators.

Glossary

adaptation body part or behavior that helps an animal survive. Soldier ants have extra-strong jaws to catch, bite, and attack.

camouflage patterns or colors that help an animal blend in with its background. Some types of toad have green-brown skin to help them hide in a backyard.

compete fight with others for something. Robins compete with other birds for space and food.

echolocation using sounds to find something. Bats use echolocation to find their way at night and to find prey.

ecosystem a place and the living things in it. A backyard ecosystem includes the grass, trees, soil, air, and the animals living in those places.

mate when male and female animals come together to produce young. After male and female spiders mate, the female lays hundreds of eggs.

niche role in an ecosystem. Owls and hawks have different niches because owls hunt by day and hawks hunt by night.

predator animal that catches and eats other animals. Bats are predators that eat insects.

prey animal that gets caught and eaten by other animals. Insects are a bat's prey.

resources water, food, and other things that animals need. Animals live in an ecosystem because it provides them with the resources they need.

silk strong thread that spiders make in their bodies. Spiders use silk to make webs and "parachutes."

territory area that an animal guards from others. An animal's territory has the food it needs as well as a space where the animal can take shelter or have young.

Want to Know More?

There is a lot to know about your backyard! These are the best places to look:

Books

- Bishop, Nic. *Backyard Detective: Critters Up Close*. New York: Scholastic, 2002.
- Parker, Steve. *Adaptation*. Chicago: Heinemann Library, 2001.
- Solway, Andrew. *What's Living in Your Backyard?* Chicago: Heinemann Library, 2004.

Websites

- http://mbgnet.mobot.org/

  Want to learn about other ecosystems? Check out this site to find out about the plants and animals that live in ecosystems beyond your backyard!

- http://www.nwf.org/backyard wildlifehabitat/

  This site from the National Wildlife Federation will give you more information about how to help create a habitat for wildlife in your backyard.

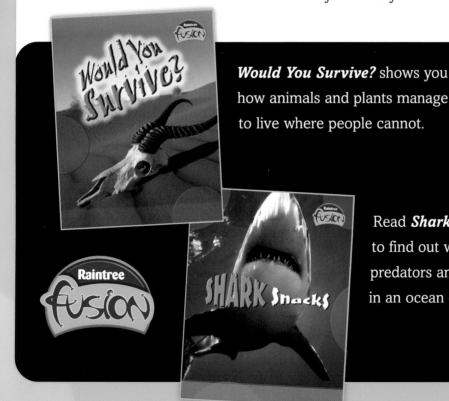

Would You Survive? shows you how animals and plants manage to live where people cannot.

Read *Shark Snacks* to find out who the predators and prey are in an ocean ecosystem.

Index